AMERICA'S MOST WINNING TEAMS™

TEXAS FOOTBALL

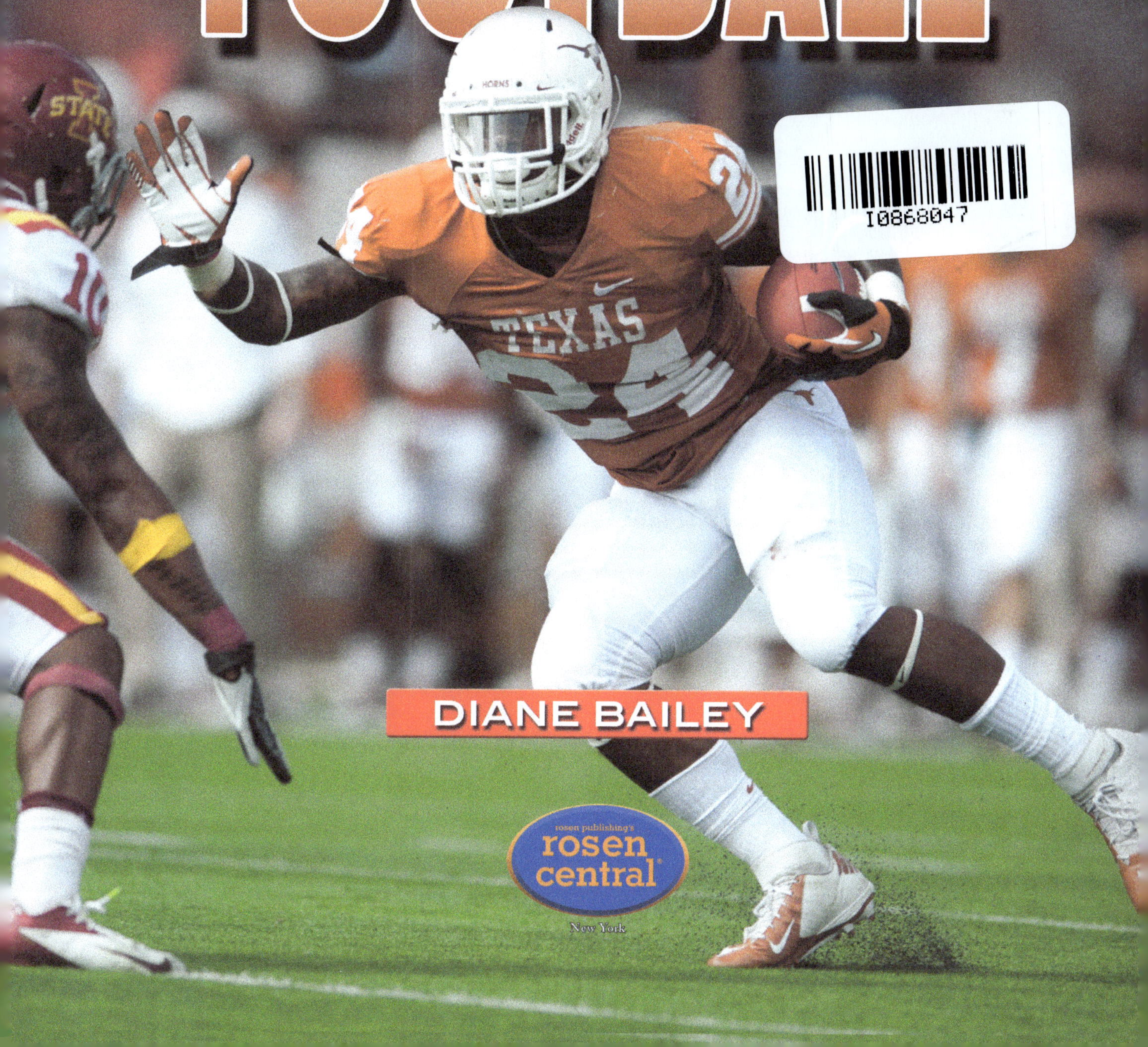

DIANE BAILEY

rosen publishing's
rosen central
New York

Published in 2014 by The Rosen Publishing Group, Inc.
29 East 21st Street, New York, NY 10010

First Edition

Library of Congress Cataloging-in-Publication Data

Bailey, Diane, 1966–.
Texas football/Diane Bailey.—1st ed.—New York: Rosen, © 2014
p. cm.—(America's most winning teams)
Includes bibliographical references and index.
ISBN: 978-1-4488-9398-0 (Library Binding)
ISBN: 978-1-4488-9442-0 (Paperback)
ISBN: 978-1-4488-9445-1 (6-pack)
1. Football—Juvenile literature. 2. Football—Awards—United States.
3. University of Texas at Austin—Football—History. 4. Texas Longhorns (Football team)—History. I. Title.
GV958.T45 .B35 2014
796.332'63

Manufactured in the United States of America

CPSIA Compliance Information: Batch #S13YA: For further information, contact Rosen Publishing, New York, New York, at 1-800-237-9932.

CONTENTS

INTRODUCTION

In Texas, football is more than something to do on a Saturday afternoon in the fall. It's a way of life. The loyalty runs deep on the "Forty Acres," the main campus of the University of Texas in Austin. On game days, the lights glow in the burnt orange of the Texas school colors. Inside Darrell K Royal-Texas Memorial Stadium, the notes of the school song, "The Eyes of Texas," echo through the one hundred thousand seats. Fans raise their hands in the air, showing the "Hook 'em Horns" hand signal.

Longhorn football started back in 1893, with a handful of players that made up the school's first team. Several hundred fans gathered to watch as the "varsity" squad—they weren't called the Longhorns yet—stunned their opponents by winning their first game.

One hundred and twenty years later, the Longhorns have racked up a few hundred more wins and collected a few million more fans. They are recognized as one of the best college football programs in the country. With more than 850 wins, Texas ranks second in the nation in overall wins. They've also claimed four national championships and dozens of conference titles. Many of their players have been inducted into the College Football Hall of Fame. Two former players—Earl Campbell and Ricky Williams—have won the Heisman Trophy, the most

The marching band takes the field at the Darrell K Royal-Texas Memorial Stadium, playing to enthusiastic fans as the University of Texas Longhorns football team gets ready for a game.

prestigious award in college football. And when these athletes leave Texas? Many have played professionally in the National Football League (NFL).

Along the way, there have been brilliant plays and unforgettable performances. There have been costly mistakes and heartbreaking moments. At the University of Texas, a football game might be celebrated, or it might be mourned. But almost everyone pays attention. When the Longhorns take the field, the "Eyes of Texas" are upon them.

CHAPTER 1

THE BOYS FROM AUSTIN

Two Texas brothers, Paul and Ray McLane, can take credit for bringing football to the University of Texas. They had gone to college in the northeast part of the country. There, football was popular at Ivy League schools such as Harvard and Yale. Back on the plains of Texas, however, the sport was not widespread.

There *was* a team in Dallas. It was undefeated and known for its brutal style of play. The players didn't mind breaking a few bones in pursuit of a win. They were willing to take on anyone who dared face them. The McLane brothers took up the challenge and put together a team. In 1893, they played Dallas.

BUILDING THE PROGRAM

The Dallas team probably expected an easy win. They had a surprise coming. In front of a couple of thousand fans, the boys from Austin beat Dallas, 18–16. Was the win just a fluke? The UT team lined up some more opponents—three—to put together its first season of four games. University students also chipped in money to hire a coach. Texas played the rest of its games, winning all four by the end of the season.

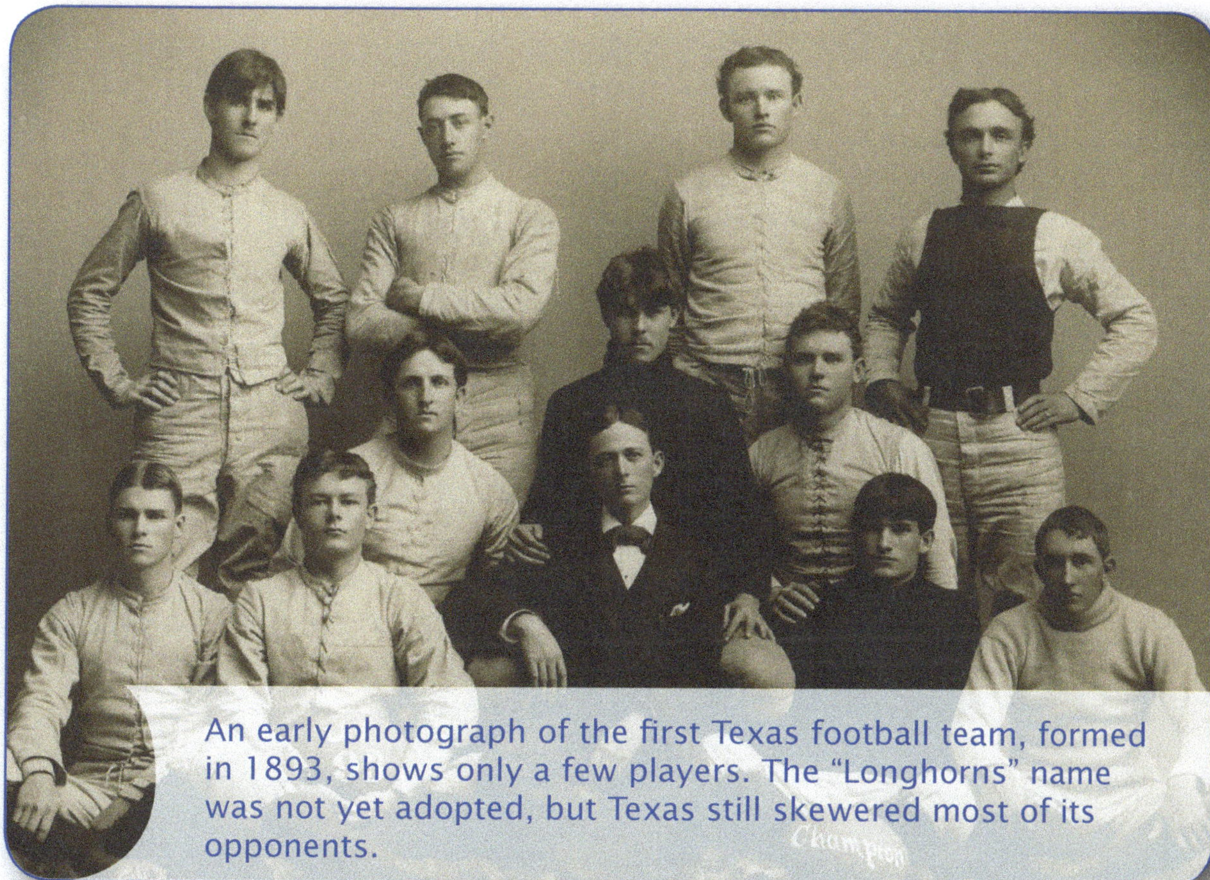

An early photograph of the first Texas football team, formed in 1893, shows only a few players. The "Longhorns" name was not yet adopted, but Texas still skewered most of its opponents.

The next year, 1894, Texas increased its schedule to seven games, including the first ever against Texas A&M University. That started a rivalry that lasted for more than a hundred years. Texas won the first six matchups without having a single point scored on them. The last game, against Missouri, broke the streak, when Texas lost 28–0. They rebounded in the next season to win all five of their games.

Over the next four decades, UT consistently expanded its schedule. They added more games and branched out to include teams outside the state. They played teams in Arkansas, Missouri, Oklahoma, Louisiana, and beyond, setting the stage for rivalries that continue to this day. From

TEXAS TRADITIONS

Texas's first, and longest-lived, rivalry was with the Texas A&M University "Aggies." Several school traditions surrounded the annual game that was played for more than one hundred years.

By the early 1900s, newspapers had nicknamed the Texas football team the "Longhorns." The longhorn is a breed of cattle that is raised in Texas. Several years later, the team adopted an actual longhorn steer as their mascot. This happened during the 1916 game against A&M. A Texas graduate scraped together $124 to buy the steer. He and some friends led it onto the sidelines at halftime, before Texas defeated A&M. The editor of the UT alumni magazine named the beast Bevo. Afterward, Bevo retired to a nearby ranch. He lived there for a few years before he was butchered and served for dinner at a UT banquet.

Another Texas ritual is the hex rally, which was first held in 1941. The Longhorns had been unable to beat the Aggies on their home turf for eighteen years. A psychic decided there was a curse at work and advised burning red candles to break the hex. Whether it was good playing or good hexing at work, the Longhorns pulled out a 23–0 win. After that, the hex rally became an annual event.

1893–1932, Texas racked up an impressive record: forty consecutive winning seasons.

GROWING PAINS

It couldn't last, of course, and it didn't. In the early 1930s, Texas football hit a rough patch. Former UT football player Clyde Littlefield had taken over coaching the team in 1927. For his first six years, Littlefield posted winning records for

Dressed in cowboy clothes, two handlers walk the Longhorn steer "Bevo" onto the field before a game. Over the years there have been several versions of "Bevo," the official name of the team mascot.

the team. But in 1933, the unthinkable happened: Texas had a losing season. The team's players lacked experience, and several of them suffered from injuries. But those excuses weren't good enough. Under pressure, Littlefield resigned. He did, however, stay with the university, becoming a successful track and field coach.

University officials chose Jack Chevigny to replace Littlefield. Chevigny led the Longhorns for three years, but the team only had a winning season in his first year. The second year, the Longhorns posted a 4–6 record. In 1936, the results were a dismal 2–6–1. As Littlefield had before him, Chevigny resigned. He is the only UT football coach to have a losing record overall.

Was Texas football doomed? One bad year was understandable, but three out of the last four was not acceptable. The athletics department began looking around for some new talent. Several years before, a man named Dana

X. Bible had been the head coach at Texas A&M. Bible was well liked. He had earned respect for his skill as a coach and for his overall good character. Texas officials decided they wanted him. To make sure Bible would accept their invitation, they offered him a salary nearly double what the president of the university earned! (Then, they had to give the president a raise.)

THE BIBLE PLAN

Bible realized that the UT football program needed an overhaul. One of his tasks was to recruit good players for the team. He reached out to the state's high schools, hoping to keep Texas talent in Texas. He also emphasized good sportsmanship and a focus on academics. The Bible plan,

THE RED RIVER RIVALRY

Texas started playing Oklahoma in 1900, but the two schools' rivalry really started in the 1940s, after World War II. The whole country had suffered economically during the war, but Oklahoma had it particularly bad. Dry weather had caused the Dust Bowl. Crops were ruined, and thousands of Oklahomans were driven into poverty. Oklahoma needed some state pride—and maybe football was the way to get it. In 1945, the university football team had lost five straight games to Texas. Oklahoma decided to turn that around. The university hired a new coach and started to fight back. The Red River Shootout, named for the river that divides the two states, was on. Since then, the two schools are nearly equally divided in wins and losses against each other.

as it was called, was solid—but it was also slow. The 1937 team went 2–6–1, and 1938 was even worse with a 1–8 record. The next year, 1939, was better. Bible coaxed a 5–4 winning record from his team. One notable game that year was against Arkansas. In the final seconds, Texas was down 13–7. It seemed like the whole thing was over. Fans started to leave the stadium. Then Texas scored a surprise touchdown to win. The win restored the confidence of the UT players. Afterward, it was called the Renaissance game because it symbolized a new start.

By 1940, Texas was reliving some of its old glory. They were also making new memories. One happened

Coach Dana Bible *(fourth from left)* assumed the head coaching job at the University of Texas in 1937. He revived the floundering team, which rose to national prominence by 1941.

Bobby Layne played fifteen seasons of professional football after his time with the University of Texas. In 1995, *Sports Illustrated* dubbed him "the Toughest Quarterback Who Ever Lived."

during the annual game against A&M. Noble Doss caught a 32-yard pass over his shoulder. It put Texas in position to score a touchdown on the next play and win the game. Later it was called "the impossible catch."

The Longhorns had become national favorites by the 1941 season. The team was ranked number one in the nation, and *Life* magazine featured them on its cover. Texas performed well, but there was a key loss to Texas Christian University. Despite high hopes, the team could not bring home a national championship.

A few years later, Texas introduced a new quarterback, Bobby Layne. Layne was a superb overall athlete. In addition to playing football, he was also a successful baseball pitcher for the school. Layne, who set a school record for passing yards, starred at the 1946 Cotton Bowl. There, he ran or passed for every one of Texas's points in a 40–27 win over Missouri.

In 1946, Dana Bible retired. He had compiled an impressive overall win record. Much of what he did never showed up on the scoreboard. Bible had also improved the physical facilities the team used and pumped up the enthusiasm of fans and supporters.

The stability that Bible had brought to Texas started to unravel once he was gone. The next coach, Blair Cherry, had four winning seasons but then resigned. Cherry said he felt too much pressure to win. Next, Ed Price took up the challenge of coaching UT football. Although he had some early success, the program began to decline in his later years. In 1956, the team managed only one win against nine losses. That was the worst record in the school's history. Price resigned, too.

It seemed the Longhorns needed a strong figure to lead them. They needed someone who loved the game and the culture—and would stick around for a little while.

CHAPTER 2

THE ROYAL TREATMENT

In 1955, the leader of the Longhorn pep squad taught fans how to extend their index and pinkie fingers to look like the horns of a steer. "Hook 'em Horns" became the rallying cry. But by 1956, few Longhorn opponents were being hooked, cooked, or booked into the records as anything except the latest team to beat Texas.

A LONGHORN LEGEND

After Ed Price stepped down, UT officials started looking for a new coach. They hoped to find one like Dana Bible, who could win on the field and take care of his players off the field. The man who fit the bill was Darrell Royal. Ironically, Royal was an Oklahoma man. He'd been born there and played college football for OU. Then he moved into coaching. Early in his career, he switched jobs often. He thought this flighty nature might keep him out of the running for the Texas job. But Texas officials took a chance on him, and it paid off. Royal stayed with the Texas program for twenty years.

As the youngest coach in college football, Royal immediately got to work. Like Bible, he focused first on getting players. College football started with high

For two decades, Coach Darrell Royal was the face of Texas Longhorns' football, leading the team to three national championships and forever changing the way the program was run.

school players, so Royal began making the rounds. He talked to coaches to find the best prospects. His down-to-earth personality was a hit across the state. Royal also turned his attention to upgrading the locker rooms and other facilities, and he made sure his athletes were doing all right in school. As for the football itself, Royal did not take a casual approach. Players were expected to train hard. Plays were practiced until perfect.

Royal's strategy worked. In his first year, the Longhorns earned a respectable record of 6–4–1. That redeemed them from the dismal numbers of the previous year. However, they did not beat their archrival, the University of Oklahoma. The next year, Royal tried again against the Sooners. Oklahoma was led by Royal's old coach, Bud Wilkinson. It was difficult for Royal to compete against his mentor. The game was close, but Texas pulled out a 15–14 win. Later, Royal called it the most important victory of his career. At the time, he was overcome with emotion. After the win, he went outside and threw up.

GET SMART

If his players couldn't succeed in school, Darrell Royal knew they couldn't succeed at football. After all, without decent grades, they wouldn't even be allowed onto the field. A few years into the job, Royal was asked if he needed some new coaches. Yes, he said, but not a football coach. Instead, Royal hired a "brain coach." Lan Hewlett was college football's first academic adviser. Hewlett made sure student athletes were paying attention to their studies and helped them if they had trouble in their classes.

MAKING A COMEBACK

President John F. Kennedy is pictured here with his wife, Jackie, the day he was assassinated. Despite the country being in mourning, the Longhorns played a scheduled game just days later.

Throughout the late 1950s and early 1960s, the Longhorns improved steadily. But they still had not won a national title. That finally changed in 1963. The team made a pact to win every game. Nine games into the season, they had. It was almost time for the annual Thanksgiving Day matchup with A&M. Then, less than a week before the game, President John F. Kennedy was assassinated in Dallas. Officials wondered if they should cancel the game. They decided not to. Not even a national tragedy could stop Texas football. A&M took an early lead, but the Longhorns rallied. They held onto their perfect winning streak. That win earned them the national championship.

Next up was a trip to the Cotton Bowl to face Navy. Despite Texas's amazing performance so far, some people still doubted the team's skill. A Pennsylvania sportswriter named Myron Cope said Texas was "the biggest fraud ever perpetrated on the football public." Texas responded with the best answer possible, by beating Navy 28–6. The Navy offense couldn't make any progress. Linebacker Tommy

Nobis and the UT defense stopped them again and again. Texas finished the year with a bowl game win, a national championship, and a perfect, undefeated season. If this was "fraud," then the Longhorns were master con men.

The early 1960s were a golden time for UT. From 1961 to 1964, the team turned in an astonishing record of 40–3–1. But then the team faltered. The next three years the team was only mediocre. To turn things around, Darrell Royal tried a new kind of offense in 1968. He rearranged his players into what was called the wishbone formation. This new strategy worked. Led by quarterback James Street, the Longhorns improved their record to 9–1–1 in 1968. The Texas attitude had returned. The team wanted to win, and they had the chops to do it.

GAME OF THE CENTURY

College football turned one hundred years old in 1969. To mark the occasion, ABC-TV decided to host a matchup between the nation's two best college teams. The game would pit Texas against one of its main rivals, the Arkansas Razorbacks (the "Hogs"). ABC made sure the game was huge. President Richard Nixon would attend. Afterward, he would award a plaque to the winner. The event was nicknamed "the Big Shootout."

Before that game, number one–ranked Texas had blasted through the first nine games of the season without even a close call. But against Arkansas, things got tough. The Longhorns fumbled almost immediately. Arkansas scored a touchdown less than a minute and a half into the game. Somehow, Texas held off Arkansas from scoring anymore in the first half. However, James Street and the rest of the offense weren't evening things up, either.

At the start of the second half, Texas turned over the ball to Arkansas again. That set the Hogs up to score their second touchdown. By the end of the third quarter, reality was sinking in. Texas was down 14–0. Unless they could make something happen, they were going to lose.

Well, that was a four-letter word.

At the start of the first quarter, Street managed a touchdown. That gave them six points. A standard extra-point kick would bring the Longhorns total to seven, but Coach Royal wasn't playing things safe. He wanted a win. So, he called for a riskier play, the two-point conversion. It worked, and Texas's total came to eight.

As the fourth quarter progressed, Texas still had to catch up. Royal made another risky decision. At one point, he decided not to try a running play, which had not been successful throughout the game. Instead, he told Street to pass the ball to Randy Peschel. Street questioned the decision, but Royal remained firm. Later, he said that, sometimes, you just suck it up and play a hunch.

It worked. Peschel caught the pass, putting Texas in position to tie the score with another touchdown. Then they made the extra kick and crept a point into the lead. Arkansas fought back, but the Texas defense wasn't going to blow it now. Texas emerged the victors, 15–14, from the "Game of the Century."

END OF AN ERA

Less than a month after the Arkansas game, the Longhorns finished the 1969 season with a win over Notre Dame at the Cotton Bowl. That gave them a perfect winning season and another national championship. It set the stage heading into 1970. Texas rolled through the year with only one

Freddie Steinmark

Shortly after undergoing surgery to remove his cancerous left leg, Freddie Steinmark attended the 1970 Cotton Bowl. He talked on the sidelines with quarterback James Street before the game.

Freddie Steinmark thought he had bruised his leg when he played in the historic game against Arkansas. But when he went into the hospital the next week, doctors delivered terrible news. Steinmark had bone cancer. His left leg had to be amputated. Steinmark showed remarkable strength. Less than three weeks later, he went to his team's bowl game against Notre Dame and cheered them on from the sidelines. Texas won, and Steinmark was awarded the game ball. Teammates remember Steinmark for his tough spirit and positive attitude. He lost his battle to cancer in 1971.

loss. They earned another national championship, the second in a row.

The 1970 championship team was also notable because it included Texas's first African American player, Julius Whittier. Up until the 1960s, Texas had a reputation for discriminating against black players. Whittier had taken a risk by accepting an offer to attend Texas. He opened the door for more black players to come to UT. A few years later, fullback Roosevelt Leaks became the school's first black all-American.

Darrell Royal had won three championships in eight years. But his glory days were coming to a close. For one thing, the rivalry with Oklahoma was getting ugly. Royal clashed with Barry Switzer, the Oklahoma coach. The two teams' annual showdown in 1976 ended in a tie. Afterward, Royal accused Switzer of spying on Texas. Royal was also just getting tired. The hard work of recruiting was starting to wear on him. His final game was against Arkansas, when he coached against his longtime friend Frank Broyles. The Longhorns won. After the game, both coaches retired. Royal ended his career with a 167–47–4 record, the winningest coach in Longhorn history.

CHAPTER 3

SUCCESSES AND SETBACKS

Darrell Royal would be a difficult man to replace. He had been more than the coach of the Longhorns football team. He was the representative of everything about it, good or bad. Most of it, of course, had been good. That's why it was surprising that UT athletic officials did not give Royal a hand in choosing who would take over for him. Mike Campbell, an assistant coach, was the man Royal would have chosen. Instead, the job went to Wyoming coach Fred Akers.

PASSING THE TORCH

In Texas, football is as much about personalities as it is about playing. Royal was adored by his players and staff, by the university's alumni and supporters, and by the thousands of loyal fans spread across the state. Akers was not able to inspire the same kind of confidence and affection. It may have been unrealistic for anyone to expect it from him.

Looking just at the numbers, Akers was a good coach. In the ten years he led UT, he won almost 75 percent of his games. In 1986, however, the Longhorns

Coach Fred Akers led the Longhorns throughout the late 1970s and early 1980s. Despite compiling an overall winning record, Akers lost his job after struggling for several years in a row.

turned in a losing record. Akers was transferred to a different job within the athletic department. But that came at the end of his career at the university. At the beginning, people still hoped Texas could repeat the success of the Royal years.

The late 1970s were promising. Akers had inherited a talented team from Royal. He had a powerful weapon in a running back named Earl Campbell. One coach said he thought Campbell had the ability to start in any position except quarterback. Akers had enough football savvy to take advantage of Campbell's talents. Immediately, he changed the Texas offensive formation. He moved Campbell to tailback and told him to get used to carrying the ball—a lot.

Akers went on to win the next nine seasons. However, he could not bring home a national championship. That was one problem. Another was the fact that Texas fans never

THE TYLER ROSE

Tyler, Texas, is a city known for growing roses. Most of those roses are flowers, but the best-known "Tyler rose" is running back Earl Campbell, who was born there. Barry Switzer, the coach of the OU Sooners, said Campbell was the only player he'd ever seen whom he believed could have gone straight from high school to be a professional football player.

Campbell did go on to play professionally for the Houston Oilers and the New Orleans Saints, but first he played four years as a Longhorn. In 1977, his final year, Campbell led the nation in the number of rushing yards and won the Heisman Trophy.

Pictured here in 1977, running back Earl Campbell was a star player for the Longhorns. He won the Heisman Trophy and went on to become the first draft pick for the NFL.

really believed in him. Perhaps he could have been forgiven one. Or the other. But not both.

The beginning of the end started at the end of 1983. Texas had gone undefeated through the regular season. But then they lost the Cotton Bowl to Georgia, in part because of mistakes by Akers. The 1984 season was mediocre. Texas got some wins, but got soundly beaten by Iowa in the Freedom Bowl. A second straight bowl game loss came at the end of the 1985 season, when Texas fell to the Air Force Academy in the Bluebonnet Bowl. By 1986, Texas couldn't beat many teams at all. For the first time in thirty years, the Longhorns ended the season with more losses than wins.

A DOWNWARD SPIRAL

That did it. Akers was out. Texas athletic officials decided to hire some homegrown talent. David McWilliams had played for Texas during the successful 1960s. He had also worked as an assistant coach under both Akers and Darrell Royal, and he was the current coach of Texas Tech.

But UT football was a mess. Loss upon loss had frustrated fans. Team morale was suffering. McWilliams had a big job to bring the team back. The first year wasn't too bad. In 1987, McWilliams helped the Longhorns to a 7–5 record. That included a win over Arkansas that was the first in Texas's history to be decided on the last play of the game. With no time left on the clock, wide receiver Tony Jones caught a touchdown pass from quarterback Bret Stafford and gave Texas the win.

The next two years weren't as good, although in 1989 Texas broke a five-year losing streak to Oklahoma. Freshman quarterback Peter Gardere made an amazing late-game effort to put the Longhorns on top. He went on to beat the

NCAA representative David Berst *(left)* speaks at a 1987 press conference. The association found several colleges and universities in the Southwest Conference guilty of rule violations.

Sooners the next three years, too. He is the only UT quarterback ever to beat Oklahoma four times.

Despite these high moments, Texas wasn't doing well overall. Then, in 1990, the Longhorns bounced back. They went 10–1 in the regular season, before falling to Miami in the Cotton Bowl. This surprise turnaround was called "Shock the Nation." Fans cheered up. Were things finally turning around? They weren't—1991 brought McWilliams's third losing season. He resigned, hoping someone else could do better.

Next up was John Mackovic. His first two seasons, 1992 and 1993, were not impressive. But 1994 was better, and

The Cotton Bowl

In the 1940s, the Cotton Bowl stadium in Dallas, Texas, became *the* place for football in the Southwest. The Cotton Bowl Classic game traditionally hosted the champion of the Southwest Conference, until that conference split up. The University of Texas Longhorns have played more games than any other school in the Cotton Bowl Classic. The annual Texas-Oklahoma game is also played at the stadium.

1995 was actually *good*. The Longhorns had a final record of 10–2–1 that year, with the second loss coming to Virginia Tech in the Sugar Bowl. They were starting to look like the team fans remembered from the old days.

In 1996, it was impossible to predict how the Longhorns would play. They played surprisingly well against top-ranked teams, beating Missouri and New Mexico State, who were both in the top ten. Then, Texas would melt down under pressure from teams that ranked much lower, such as Oklahoma and Oklahoma State. At the end of the season, Texas faced number three Nebraska to battle for the championship of the newly formed Big 12 Conference. With a small lead late in the first quarter, quarterback James Brown found an opening to pass for 61 yards. That set up running back Priest Holmes to score another touchdown. That cemented the win. Texas claimed the 1996 conference championship.

Then came 1997, and it was a disaster. The most humiliating moment came during the season's second game, against UCLA. Texas put only three points on the board, compared to UCLA's 66. The game was nicknamed

Coach Darrell Royal is pictured with Texas players, including Julius Whittier *(far left)*, a backup offensive lineman. In 1970, Whittier became the first black player on a national championship team.

"Rout 66," a pun off of the famous Route 66 highway that runs through Texas. Texas limped through the rest of the season, logging only four wins. It was the worst season record in more than half a century. John Mackovic would not be invited back.

SCANDAL IN THE SOUTHWEST

The 1980s and 1990s were difficult times for college football throughout the country, and particularly in the Southwest Conference (SWC). There was a lot of pressure to attract "blue-chip" recruits—the best high school players.

This had led to unethical and illegal practices among some college coaches.

By law, college athletes cannot be paid to play. It is also not permitted to give them gifts, such as cars, as compensation for their playing. In the late 1980s, the National Collegiate Athletic Association (NCAA) found that many schools, including the University of Texas, were guilty of breaking some of the rules. The worst offender was Southern Methodist University (SMU). The NCAA punished the school by banning it from football entirely in 1987. SMU opted to sit out a second year, 1988.

The scandal made the conference look bad. In addition, potential recruits opted to attend schools that weren't in danger of getting in trouble. With many of the best players going out of state, the quality of the teams suffered. By the mid-1990s, the whole situation was such a mess that the Southwest Conference broke up. Teams were reshuffled, and Texas ended up in the newly formed Big 12 Conference.

The times were changing. The new time was one for Texas to spiff up its image. And beyond that, it was time to get a good coach who could help the team win.

CHAPTER 4

ORANGE, WHITE, AND BROWN

Texas had been national champions three times in its history. The last one had come nearly thirty years earlier, before any of the current players had even been born. Was it possible to recruit the talent and recreate the team spirit that Darrell Royal had? UT wanted someone who understood football, but also someone who understood Texas.

MACK TO MACK

Mack Brown wasn't a Texas native—he was raised in Tennessee. He wasn't even a Texas resident—he was coaching in North Carolina. But he took to the job immediately. He oozed the good-natured, relaxed personality that Texans liked. And, he got support from the one man whose word still carried a lot of weight: Darrell Royal.

When Brown took over in 1998, he said the words that everyone wanted to hear: "It's not a question of 'if,'" he said. "It's a question of 'when.'" "It" meant the big one—a national championship. He also told his new team that he was not interested in "rebuilding."

Longhorns coach Mack Brown has spent plenty of time on the sidelines of the Rose Bowl. Here he shouts encouragement to players during a 2011 game against the UCLA Bruins.

That often meant a long losing streak as new players learned the ropes. Instead, he told the demoralized Longhorns, "We want to win next year."

Brown hit the road, talking to UT supporters and alumni. He also worked to build bridges with the state's high school coaches. When he was hired, there were only a couple of months left before high school players made their commitments to colleges. Brown had a huge task to try and get some of them to come to the University of Texas. In the end, he signed eighteen players, all from Texas. Many of them had been identified as the state's top players.

COACH FEBRUARY

Brown helped Texas post respectable, if not stellar, records for his first three years. In 2001, Texas showed more promise. In the first nine games, the team had only one loss, to Oklahoma. Even so, Texas was not a strong candidate for the conference championship. Then Oklahoma stumbled. The Sooners lost to their in-state rival, Oklahoma State. Suddenly, Texas was back in the running. In another dash of luck, it turned out they would face Colorado. They'd already beaten Colorado earlier in the season.

There would not be a repeat of that earlier game. Texas quarterback Chris Simms struggled. By the time Brown replaced him with Major Applewhite, too much damage had been done. Texas lost. The Longhorns did win the Holiday Bowl a few weeks later, but the Texas faithful were still stinging from the loss of the conference championship.

RICKY WILLIAMS

Not much could stop Ricky Williams. The running back, a junior, was a bright spot on the Longhorn team in 1997 and a candidate for the Heisman Trophy. But that was a frustrating year for Texas. Williams didn't win the Heisman. And even with Williams's help, the Longhorns didn't win many games. The NFL was ready to draft Williams, but in early 1998, he surprised many people. He announced he would not go pro—at least not yet. Instead, he said loyalty was more important than money, and that he would return for his senior year and play under Mack Brown. The next season, Williams did win the Heisman.

Running back Ricky Williams stayed for another year with Texas after Coach Mack Brown took over the team in 1998. Like his predecessor Earl Campbell, he took home the Heisman Trophy.

Brown's ability to recruit top players was noted, but there was a problem. Despite the team's talented players, they weren't winning the big games. Brown's critics nicknamed him "Coach February." That meant he could sign promising candidates during the recruitment season (February). But when autumn rolled around and it was time to play, the wins slipped away. Texas fans were getting antsy. Maybe Brown wasn't the right man, after all.

But 2002 and 2003 were both good seasons, with trips to bowl games both times. Then, in 2004, Texas had a great year. The only loss during the regular season came to Oklahoma. The Longhorns earned a trip to the granddaddy of all the bowl games: the Rose Bowl, held in Pasadena, California. There, Texas would play the Michigan Wolverines.

RUN FOR THE ROSES

Texas and Michigan seemed evenly matched in the game. First Texas scored a touchdown. Then Michigan responded.

TEXAS TRAGEDY

In the competition with the Longhorns, the Aggies of Texas A&M had their own tradition. Before the annual game against Texas, they held a massive bonfire at a pep rally. In 1999, the bonfire ended in a tragedy. It collapsed while being built and killed several people. Fans for both schools mourned the loss. When A&M won the game, few UT fans were unhappy. The two schools might be archrivals, but they were all Texans.

At the 2005 Rose Bowl, the Texas Longhorns line up as they prepare to defend against the Michigan Wolverines. Texas defeated Michigan on the final play of the game.

Texas scored again. So did Michigan. At halftime, the score was tied at 14–14. In the second half, the scoring came fast and furious. Both teams made a touchdown to tie at 21–21. Then Michigan leaped ahead with a touchdown and a field goal. Now the Wolverines had a ten-point lead. Texas clawed back with another touchdown, but Michigan kept the lead out of reach with a field goal. Texas scored another touchdown, putting them ahead 35–34, but Michigan kicked yet another field goal to leapfrog over Texas to a 37–35 lead.

Texas had to score again. Quarterback Vince Young ran the ball close to the end zone, but with half a minute left to play, the Longhorns decided to go for a field goal. They let the clock run down until only two seconds remained. Then kicker Dusty Mangum came in. Michigan called time-outs, trying to make Mangum nervous. But he waited patiently for his chance. When it was time, he went in, kicked a 37-yard field goal, and gave Texas the win. It was the first time the Rose Bowl had been won on the final play.

ROSE BOWL, REPEATED

Coming off the magnificent Rose Bowl win, Texas steamrolled through their 2005 schedule. They finished the season undefeated. Four of those games were won by more than fifty points! No one, it seemed, could stop Texas.

The team showed that in their second game of the season, against Ohio State. Late in the fourth quarter, Vince Young passed the ball to receiver Limas Sweed. Sweed then scored the winning touchdown. That game marked Texas's first win in six years against a top ten team. It also made people think that the Longhorns had a chance at a conference title, and maybe even a national championship. The momentum continued through the season. Texas finished the season undefeated and earned another trip to the Rose Bowl.

On New Year's Day in 2006, the Longhorns would play for the national championship against the University of Southern California. It would be a tough game. USC was looking for their third straight national title and was favored to beat Texas.

But Vince Young had other ideas. He had recently lost in the voting for the Heisman Trophy. He did not want to lose to USC, too. Young played an amazing game. He rushed for 200 yards, passed for 267 yards, and scored three touchdowns. His last touchdown came with only

Texas players celebrate after they win the Rose Bowl for the second year in a row in 2006. The Longhorns beat the University of Southern California to take home the national championship.

nineteen seconds left in the game. It put Texas into the lead, and Texas won, 41–38. The Longhorns had their first national championship in more than thirty-five years.

NEW HURDLES

The next few years were not as successful for Texas. In 2007, the team suffered when Brown suspended several players who had gotten into trouble for breaking the law. By 2009, the Longhorns rebounded. It helped that they had quarterback Colt McCoy. He eventually became the NCAA's winningest quarterback. Texas went undefeated in the regular season and beat Nebraska to take home the Big 12 championship. But several key players left in 2010, pulling the Longhorns down to a losing record of 5–7. The 2011 team posted an improved record of 8–5.

In 2012, there was a notable change. Texas A&M was not on the schedule. The rivalry that had lasted more than a century had ended. The decision disappointed some fans. Others thought it showed that Texas was entering a new era, and that the school was ready to take on new challenges.

Over the last century, Texas has run, passed, and tackled its way through the changes that have come to college football. It hasn't always been easy, or fast, but Texas is stubborn. One way or another, they will horn their way to the top.

TIMELINE

1893: The University of Texas's football team plays its first game, against a Dallas city team. Texas wins.

1900: Texas first plays the University of Oklahoma, beginning a long-term rivalry.

1916: The Longhorns acquire a steer named Bevo as the team mascot.

1933: Texas has its first losing season, after forty consecutive winning ones.

1937: Coach Dana X. Bible accepts the job as head coach of UT football.

1941: The Longhorn team is featured on the cover of *Life* magazine; the first hex rally, as part of the lead-up to the annual matchup against rival Texas A&M, is held.

1955: "Hook 'em Horns" becomes the team's rallying cry

1957: Darrell Royal becomes the Longhorns' head coach.

1963: The Longhorns win their first national championship.

1968: Darrell Royal introduces a new offensive strategy with the wishbone formation.

1969: The Longhorns win a second national title; they play the Game of the Century against the University of Arkansas Razorbacks.

1970: Texas wins the national championship for the second year in a row, making it the third overall.

1977: Running back Earl Campbell wins the Heisman Trophy, the first for the University of Texas.

1985: Texas loses its second straight bowl game with a loss to the Air Force.

1989: Freshman quarterback Peter Gardere breaks a five-year losing streak against the University of Oklahoma. He goes on to lead victories against the Sooners for the next three years.

1990: The Longhorns achieve a surprise 10–1 record in a season nicknamed "Shock the Nation."

1996: Texas wins the first conference championship of the newly formed Big 12 Conference.

1998: Mack Brown takes over as head coach; Ricky Williams wins the Heisman Trophy.

2005: Texas beats the Michigan Wolverines at the Rose Bowl.

2006: Texas beats USC at the Rose Bowl to win its fourth national title.

2009: Quarterback Colt McCoy leads Texas to an undefeated regular season and is named the NCAA's Quarterback of the Year.

2012: For the first time in more than a century, Texas does not play its longstanding rival Texas A&M.

GLOSSARY

assassinate To kill someone for political reasons.

compensation Money, material possessions, or other rewards received in return for a service.

discriminate To treat people in a negative or unfair manner based on their inherent characteristics, such as race or religion.

falter To hesitate, or not be able to complete something.

fluke An accidental occurrence, often with an unexpected result.

hex A spell.

inducted Formally accepted into an organization.

Ivy League A collection of prestigious colleges in the northeast United States, named because of the ivy on the walls of the buildings.

longhorn A species of cattle that thrives in the Texas climate.

mediocre Average, unimpressive.

pact An agreement or deal.

perpetrate To commit an action.

prestigious Respected, important.

rush In football, the act of running with the ball.

savvy Smart, sensible.

suspend To temporarily stop or reject something.

two-point conversion A play in football where a one-point kick is changed into a running play with the possibility of two points.

FOR MORE INFORMATION

Big 12 Conference
400 East John Carpenter Freeway
Irving, TX 75062
(469) 524-1000
Web site: http://www.big12sports.com

The Big 12 Conference is comprised of ten colleges, including the University of Texas. The organization oversees play within the conference and organizes competitions.

College Football Hall of Fame
111 South St. Joseph Street
South Bend, IN 46601
(574) 235-9999
Web site: http://www.collegefootball.org

The College Football Hall of Fame recognizes players who have demonstrated outstanding achievements during their college careers.

Heisman Memorial Trophy
111 Broadway, Suite 103A
New York, NY 10006
(212) 425-7000
Web site: http://www.heisman.com/index.php

The Heisman Trophy is awarded annually to college football's most outstanding player. The Heisman Trust, which administers the award, is also a charity that supports amateur athletics.

National Collegiate Athletic Association (NCAA)
700 W. Washington Street
P.O. Box 6222

Indianapolis, IN 46206-6222

(317) 917-6222

Web site: http://www.ncaa.org

The NCAA represents student athletes in all college sports and across all levels of play. Each of its three divisions creates and enforces regulations and organizes competitive play among its members.

University of Texas Athletics

The University of Texas at Austin

P.O. Box 7399

Austin, TX 78713-7399

Web site: http://www.texassports.com

The athletics department for the University of Texas at Austin manages the college's sports teams and maintains a comprehensive Web site with information about players and games.

WEB SITES

Due to the changing nature of Internet links, Rosen Publishing has developed an online list of Web sites related to the subject of this book. This site is updated regularly. Please use this link to access the list:

http://www.rosenlinks.com/AMWT/TXFB

FOR FURTHER READING

Berman, Len. *The Greatest Moments in Sports: Upsets and Underdogs*. Naperville, IL: Sourcebooks Jabberwocky, 2012.

Biskup, Agnieszka. *Football: How It Works*. Mankato, MN: Capstone Press, 2010.

Christopher, Matt, and Stephanie Peters. *The Greatest Sports Team Rivalries*. New York, NY: Little, Brown Books for Young Readers, 2012.

DeCock, Luke. *Great Teams in College Football History*. Mankato, MN: Heinemann-Raintree, 2005.

Frederick, Shane Gerald. *The Best of Everything Football Book*. Mankato, MN: Capstone Press, 2011.

Jacobs, Greg. *The Everything Kids' Football Book: The All-Time Greats, Legendary Teams, Today's Superstars—and Tips on Playing Like a Pro*. Avon, MA: Adams Media, 2010.

Rappoport, Ken. *Michigan Wolverines*. Minneapolis, MN: ABDO Publishing Company, 2012.

Roselius, J. Chris. *Texas Longhorns*. Minneapolis, MN: ABDO Publishing Company, 2012.

Sports Illustrated Kids 1st and 10: Top Ten Lists of Everything in Football. New York, NY: Sports Illustrated, 2011.

Stewart, Mark. *The Texas Longhorns*. Chicago, IL: Norwood House Press, 2010.

Stewart, Mark, and Mike Kennedy. *Touchdown: The Power and Precision of Football's Perfect Play*. Minneapolis, MN: Millbrook Press, 2009.

BIBLIOGRAPHY

Barnhouse, Wendell. *Longhorns Handbook: Stories, Stats and Stuff About Texas Football*. Wichita, KS: The Wichita Eagle and Beacon Publishing Co., 1996.

Hawthorne, Bobby. *Longhorn Football: An Illustrated History*. Austin, TX: University of Texas Press, 2007.

Ketchum, Geoff. *The Die-Hard Fan's Guide to Longhorn Football*. Washington, DC: Regnery Publishing, Inc., 2008.

Maher, John, and Kirk Bohls. *Long Live the Longhorns! 100 Years of Texas Football*. New York, NY: St. Martin's Press, 1993.

Maysel, Lou. *Here Come the Texas Longhorns, 1893–1970*. Fort Worth, TX: Stadium Publishing Company, 1970.

Pennington, Richard. *Texas Longhorns Football History A to Z*. Hingham, MA: Maple Street Press, 2008.

Samelson, Ken, ed. *Echoes of Texas Football: The Greatest Stories Ever Told*. Chicago, IL: Triumph Books, 2006.

Schoor, Gene. *100 Years of Texas Longhorn Football*. Dallas, TX: Taylor Publishing Company, 1993.

Sharpe, Wilton. *Longhorn Madness: Great Eras in Texas Football*. Nashville, TN: Cumberland House Publishing, Inc., 2006.

Shropshire, Mike. *Runnin' with the Big Dogs*. New York, NY: HarperCollins, 2006.

Statesman.com. "Take Tens: Horns, Aggies Rivalry Defined by Great Games, Players, Moments, Traditions." November 23, 2011. Retrieved June 16, 2012 (http://www.statesman.com/sports/longhorns/take-tens-horns-aggies-rivalry-defined-by-great-1991584.html).

Wangrin, Mark. *Horns! A History*. New York, NY: Fireside, 2006.

INDEX

ABOUT THE AUTHOR

Diane Bailey has written about twenty-five nonfiction books for teens, on subjects ranging from sports to states to celebrities. Her first novel, *Murder a Cappella*, a murder mystery, was published in 2012. Bailey also works as an editor for other children's authors. She has two sons and two dogs and lives in Kansas.

PHOTO CREDITS

Cover, p.1 Cooper Neill/Getty Images; back cover (goal post) David Lee/Shutterstock.com; p. 4 Greg Nelson/Sports Illustrated/Getty Images; p. 5 Darren Carroll/Sports Illustrated; pp. 6, 14, 22, 31 (helmet) from photo by Cooper Neill/Getty Images; p. 7 University of Texas Athletics; p. 9 Jed Jacobsohn/Getty Images; p. 11 Allan Grant/Time & Life Pictures/Getty Images; pp. 12, 20, 23, 27, 38 © AP Images; p. 15 Art Shay/Sports Illustrated/Getty Images; p. 17 Art Rickerby/Time & Life Pictures/Getty Images; p. 25 Sporting News Archive/Getty Images; p. 29 Mark Graham/The New York Times/Redux Pictures; p. 32 Harry How/Getty Images; p. 34 Brian Bahr/Getty Images; p. 36 Stephen Dunn/Getty Images; multiple interior page borders and boxed text backgrounds (football) Nickola_Che/Shutterstock.com; back cover and multiple interior pages background (abstract pattern) © iStockphoto.com/Che McPherson.

Designer: Brian Garvey; Editor: Bethany Bryan;
Photo Researcher: Marty Levick